by Iain Gray

Lang**Syne**
PUBLISHING

WRITING *to* REMEMBER

79 Main Street, Newtongrange,
Midlothian EH22 4NA
Tel: 0131 344 0414   Fax: 0845 075 6085
E-mail: info@lang-syne.co.uk
www.langsyneshop.co.uk

Design by Dorothy Meikle
Printed by Printwell Ltd
© Lang Syne Publishers Ltd 2022

All rights reserved. No part of this publication may be reproduced, stored or introduced into a retrieval system, or transmitted in any form or by any means (electronic, mechanical, photocopying, recording or otherwise) without the prior written permission of Lang Syne Publishers Ltd.

ISBN 978-1-85217-519-1

Rogers

MOTTO:
We and ours to God
(and)
Act justly, and fear nothing.

CREST:
A demi-stag.

NAME variations include:
Rodger
Rodgers
Roger

Chapter one:

The origins of popular surnames

by George Forbes and Iain Gray

If you don't know where you came from, you won't know where you're going **is a frequently quoted observation and one that has a particular resonance today when there has been a marked upsurge in interest in genealogy, with increasing numbers of people curious to trace their family roots.**

Main sources for genealogical research include census returns and official records of births, marriages and deaths – and the key to unlocking the detail they contain is obviously a family surname, one that has been 'inherited' and passed from generation to generation.

No matter our station in life, we all have a surname – but it was not until about the middle of the fourteenth century that the practice of being identified by a particular surname became commonly established throughout the British Isles.

Previous to this, it was normal for a person to be identified through the use of only a forename.

But as population gradually increased and there were many more people with the same forename, surnames were adopted to distinguish one person, or community, from another.

Many common English surnames are patronymic in origin, meaning they stem from the forename of one's father – with 'Johnson,' for example, indicating 'son of John.'

It was the Normans, in the wake of their eleventh century conquest of Anglo-Saxon England, a pivotal moment in the nation's history, who first brought surnames into usage – although it was a gradual process.

For the Normans, these were names initially based on the title of their estates, local villages and chateaux in France to distinguish and identify these landholdings.

Such grand descriptions also helped enhance the prestige of these warlords and generally glorify their lofty positions high above the humble serfs slaving away below in the pecking order who had only single names, often with Biblical connotations as in Pierre and Jacques.

The only descriptive distinctions among the peasantry concerned their occupations, like 'Pierre the swineherd' or 'Jacques the ferryman.'

Roots of surnames that came into usage in England not only included Norman-French, but also Old French, Old Norse, Old English, Middle English, German, Latin, Greek, Hebrew and the Gaelic languages of the Celts.

The Normans themselves were originally Vikings, or 'Northmen', who raided, colonised and eventually settled down around the French coastline.

They had sailed up the Seine in their longboats in 900AD under their ferocious leader Rollo and ruled the roost in north eastern France before sailing over to conquer England in 1066 under Duke William of Normandy – better known to posterity as William the Conqueror, or King William I of England.

Granted lands in the newly-conquered England, some of their descendants later acquired territories in Wales, Scotland and Ireland – taking not only their own surnames, but also the practice of adopting a surname, with them.

But it was in England where Norman rule and custom first impacted, particularly in relation to the adoption of surnames.

This is reflected in the famous *Domesday Book*, a massive survey of much of England and Wales, ordered by William I, to determine who owned what, what it was worth and therefore how much they were liable to pay in taxes to the voracious Royal Exchequer.

Completed in 1086 and now held in the National Archives in Kew, London, 'Domesday' was an Old English word meaning 'Day of Judgement.'

This was because, in the words of one contemporary chronicler, "its decisions, like those of the Last Judgement, are unalterable."

It had been a requirement of all those English landholders – from the richest to the poorest – that they identify themselves for the purposes of the survey and for future reference by means of a surname.

This is why the *Domesday Book*, although written in Latin as was the practice for several centuries with both civic and ecclesiastical records, is an invaluable source for the early appearance of a wide range of English surnames.

Several of these names were coined in connection with occupations.

These include Baker and Smith, while Cooks, Chamberlains, Constables and Porters were to be found carrying out duties in large medieval households.

The church's influence can be found in names such as Bishop, Friar and Monk while the popular name of Bennett derives from the late fifth to mid-sixth century Saint Benedict, founder of the Benedictine order of monks.

The early medical profession is represented by Barber, while businessmen produced names that include Merchant and Sellers.

Down at the village watermill, the names that cropped up included Millar/Miller, Walker and Fuller, while other self-explanatory trades included Cooper, Tailor, Mason and Wright.

Even the scenery was utilised as in Moor, Hill, Wood and Forrest – while the hunt and the chase supplied names that include Hunter, Falconer, Fowler and Fox.

Colours are also a source of popular surnames, as in Black, Brown, Gray/Grey, Green and White, and would have denoted the colour of the clothing the person habitually wore or, apart from the obvious exception of 'Green', one's hair colouring or even complexion.

The surname Red developed into Reid, while

Blue was rare and no-one wanted to be associated with yellow.

Rather self-important individuals took surnames that include Goodman and Wiseman, while physical attributes crept into surnames such as Small and Little.

Many families proudly boast the heraldic device known as a Coat of Arms, as featured on our front cover.

The central motif of the Coat of Arms would originally have been what was borne on the shield of a warrior to distinguish himself from others on the battlefield.

Not featured on the Coat of Arms, but highlighted on page three, is the family motto and related crest – with the latter frequently different from the central motif.

Adding further variety to the rich cultural heritage that is represented by surnames is the appearance in recent times in lists of the 100 most common names found in England of ones that include Khan, Patel and Singh – names that have proud roots in the vast sub-continent of India.

Echoes of a far distant past can still be found in our surnames and they can be borne with pride in commemoration of our forebears.

Chapter two:

Martial origins

A name of truly warlike roots, 'Rogers', meaning 'son of Roger', derives from the popular given name of 'Roger' which, in turn, derives from the Germanic 'hrothgar', meaning 'fame-spear.'

Also indicating 'prowess with a spear', the name was originally bestowed on someone noted for their skill as a soldier.

One of its spelling variants is 'Rodgers' – particularly prevalent in Scotland, Wales and southern and western England – and whose bearers have their own proud and separate history.

In Ireland, meanwhile, the name is an Anglicisation of the Gaelic 'MacRuaidhrí ' meaning 'son of the red king.'

Flowing through the veins of many bearers of the name today may well be the blood of those Germanic tribes who invaded and first settled in the south and east of the island of Britain from about the early fifth century.

Known as the Anglo-Saxons, they were composed of the Jutes, from the area of the Jutland

Peninsula in modern Denmark, the Saxons from Lower Saxony, in modern Germany and the Angles from the Angeln area of Germany.

It was the Angles who gave the name 'Engla land', or 'Aengla land' – better known as 'England.'

They held sway in what became England from approximately 550 until the Norman Conquest of 1066, with the main kingdoms those of Sussex, Wessex, Northumbria, Mercia, Kent, East Anglia and Essex.

Whoever controlled the most powerful of these kingdoms was tacitly recognised as overall 'king' – one of the most noted being Alfred the Great, King of Wessex from 871 to 899.

It was during his reign that the famous *Anglo-Saxon Chronicle* was compiled – an invaluable source of Anglo-Saxon history – while Alfred was designated in early documents as *Rex Anglorum Saxonum*, King of the English Saxons.

Other important Anglo-Saxon works include the epic *Beowulf* and the seventh century *Caedmon's Hymn*.

Through the Anglo-Saxons, the language known as Old English developed, later transforming from the eleventh century into Middle English –

sources from which many popular English surnames of today, such as Rogers, derive.

The name is first found in Cornwall, while a Henry Rogeres is recorded in Worcestershire in 1237, a Richard Roger in Kent in 1263 and William Rogger in Sussex in 1296.

It is a name that features prominently in the frequently turbulent historical record.

Born in Birmingham in 1500, John Rogers was the clergyman and Biblical translator who has the dubious distinction of having been the first Protestant martyr during the reign from 1553 to 1558 of the Catholic Queen Mary I – also known to posterity as 'Bloody Mary.'

The son of a lorimer – as makers of equipment for horses and riders were known – he served from 1532 to 1534 as rector of the Church of Holy Trinity the Less, in London, after graduating from Cambridge University.

Appointed chaplain to the English merchants of the Company of Merchant Adventurers in Antwerp, he made the acquaintance of the Biblical translator William Tyndale – and it was under his influence that he abandoned the Roman Catholic faith in favour of Protestantism.

Tyndale died in 1536, and Rogers took over the onerous task of completion of his translation of sections of the Old Testament – with much of his work later forming an important basis for the King James Version of the Bible.

Later returning to his native England, he incurred the wrath of the authorities by preaching against what he perceived as "pestilent Popery, idolatry and superstition."

Sentenced to death after being convicted of "heretically denying the Christian character of the Church of Rome and the real presence of the Sacrament", he was burned at the stake in February of 1555 – making him the first Protestant martyr under Mary.

During the bitter seventeenth century English Civil War, John Rogers was the physician and dissenting Protestant preacher born in 1627 in Messing, Essex.

The Catholic monarch Charles I had incurred the wrath of Parliament by his insistence on the 'divine right' of kings, and added to this was Parliament's fear of Catholic 'subversion' against the state and the king's stubborn refusal to grant demands for religious and constitutional concessions.

Matters came to a head with the outbreak of the Civil War in 1642, with Parliamentary forces, known as the New Model Army and commanded by Oliver Cromwell and Sir Thomas Fairfax, arrayed against the Royalist army of the king.

In what became an increasingly bloody and complex conflict, spreading to Scotland and Ireland and with rapidly shifting loyalties on both sides, the king was eventually captured and executed in January of 1649 on the orders of Parliament.

In the turmoil that followed his execution, through the grim ordeal of being beheaded, and the further consolidation of power by Cromwell, a number of dissenting, or 'non-conformist' groups sprang up.

Among them were the Fifth Monarchists, or Fifth Monarchy, and one of their leading lights was John Rogers.

Taking their name from a prophecy in the Book of Daniel that the four ancient monarchies of Babylonia, Persia, Macedonia and Rome would precede the 'Fifth Monarchy' – the kingdom of Christ, they also believed that the year 1666 – referring to the Biblical number of the 'Great Beast' – would end the earthly rule of 'carnal' human beings.

Preaching that Cromwell and his clique were among these 'carnal' beings, Rogers was arrested and placed in confinement a number of times.

Cromwell died in 1658, while Charles II was restored to the throne in 1660 – and it is around this time that Rogers moved to the Netherlands, returning to England in 1664.

He then disappears from the historical record, with not even his date of death known.

One of his sons, however, was the politician and merchant Sir John Rogers, born in 1649.

Serving in the House of Commons from 1698 to 1700 as Member of Parliament (MP) for Plymouth, he died in 1710 after having been created 1st Baronet of Wisdome, in the County of Devon.

Chapter three:

Adventurous spirits

One particularly colourful bearer of the Rogers name was the English sea captain Woodes Rogers, famed for having rescued the shipwrecked Scot Alexander Selkirk – who became the inspiration for Daniel Defoe's novel *Robinson Crusoe*.

Born in about 1679 in Poole into a wealthy seafaring family, he was left in control of his father's shipping interests following his death when Rogers was aged in his mid-twenties.

Taking to the high seas, he became a privateer, capturing a number of prize Spanish vessels during the 1702 to 1713 War of the Spanish Succession.

In February of 1709, during a three-year expedition circumnavigating the globe, Rogers and an accompanying frigate headed for Juan Fernandez Island in the Pacific to replenish supplies of food and water.

Approaching the island, they spotted a fire and, cautiously venturing ashore for fear that the blaze may have been lit by a Spanish shore party, discovered Alexander Selkirk, who had been marooned there for four years.

Rogers wrote an account of his meeting with Selkirk, and this was subsequently passed on to his good friend Daniel Defoe.

It recorded how the Scot was "wild-looking and wearing goatskins ... he had with him his clothes and bedding, with a firelock, some powder, bullets and tobacco, a hatchet, a knife, a kettle, a Bible and books."

Following his rescue, Selkirk joined Rogers and his crew for the remainder of their circumnavigation of the globe.

Capturing a number of Spanish vessels, it was one of these, placed under the command of Simon Hatley, that later became the subject of the poet Samuel Taylor Coleridge's' *The Rhyme of the Ancient Mariner*.

This was partly based on an incident when Hatley shot an albatross in hope of better winds as his vessel lay becalmed.

Serving for a time as first Governor of the Bahamas, Rogers died in 1732.

A number of other intrepid characters have also borne the Rogers name.

A pioneer of the California Gold Rush of 1848 to 1855, John Haney Rogers, born in 1822 in Tennessee, is remembered for the gruelling 500-mile round-trip he made in late 1849 and early 1850 to save the lives of fellow members of a party heading for the gold fields.

Furnished with what turned out to be a hopelessly inaccurate map that purported to show a route from Salt Lake City, Utah, to California, the party eventually found themselves stranded in the inhospitable desert wastes of what is aptly known as Death Valley.

Vainly searching for a pass through the Panamint Range of mountains, and on the brink of starvation, John Rogers and William Lewis Manly set off in search of help.

Trekking for two weeks through the Mojave Desert, the exhausted pair eventually stumbled upon the settlement of Rancho San Francisco, about 30 miles northeast of the present-day city of Los Angeles.

Buying a pair of horses and a mule loaded with vital provisions, they made it back to their stranded party. Rogers and Manly were then able to lead them to safety.

Rogers subsequently worked for a time in gold mining and then as a farmer before his death in 1906 in Merced, California.

Born in 1829 in Massachusetts, Albert Bowman Rogers was the American surveyor better known as Major A. B. Rogers.

Having served with the U.S. Cavalry during the Indian Wars, it was while working for the Canadian Pacific Railway that in 1882 he discovered what was later named in his honour as the Rogers Pass.

Located in Montana and a route over what is known as the Continental Divide, it is now the highway route between Great Falls and Missoula known as Montana Highway 200.

Rogers died after falling from his horse while surveying a route in 1909 for the Great Northern Railway, near Coeur d'Alene, Idaho.

Bearers of the Rogers name have also made their mark as highly successful entrepreneurs.

Born in 1840 in Mattapoisett, Massachusetts, Henry Huddleston Rogers was one of the founders of what became the mighty Standard Oil Company.

Born into a family who were descended from the seventeenth century *Mayflower* settlers from

England, Rogers made the basis of his fortune in 1861 when he and his friend and business partner Charles P. Ellis pooled their resources to create what eventually became Standard Oil; he died in 1909.

An inductee of Canada's Telecommunications Hall of Fame, along with his father, Edward S. Rogers, Sr., Edwards Samuel Rogers, Jr., born in Toronto in 1933, was the businessman better known as Ted Rogers.

Rated before his death in 2008 as the fifth richest person in Canada in terms of net worth, he was in charge of Rogers Communications, established in 1967, and one of Canada's biggest media conglomerates.

In addition to his radio and cable television interests, Rogers also had a number of sporting interests that included ownership of the Toronto Blue Jays Major League Baseball Team.

As a philanthropist, he and his wife Loretta Rogers donated $15million in 2007 to Ryerson University for the establishment of the Ted Rogers School of Management.

In keeping with the origins of the Rogers name as a description of a skilled warrior, three of its bearers have been recipients of the Victoria Cross

(VC), the highest award for valour in the face of enemy action for British and Commonwealth forces.

Born in Dublin in 1834, Robert Rogers was a recipient of the honour during the 1856 to 1860 Second Opium War in China.

He had been a lieutenant in the 44th Regiment of Foot when, in August of 1860 at Taku Forts, along with two others who also received the honour, he managed to storm a heavily fortified enemy position; later achieving the rank of major general, he died in 1895.

An Australian recipient of the VC during the Second Boer War of 1899 to 1902, James Rogers was born in 1875 in Echuca, Victoria.

A sergeant in the South African Constabulary, South African Forces, it was in June of 1901 at Thabu 'Nchu that, following a skirmish with a party of about 60 Boers, he was able to rescue a number of wounded comrades and take them back to the safety of their lines.

Serving during the First World War and wounded at Anzac Cove, Gallipoli, he died in 1961; his VC is now displayed at the Australian War Museum, Canberra.

Born in Bristol in 1919, Maurice Rogers was

a posthumous recipient of the VC during the Second World War.

A sergeant in the 2nd Battalion, The Wiltshire Regiment, during the battle of Anzio, in Italy, in August of 1944, he was shot and killed after a successful single-handed assault on an enemy position; his VC is now on display at The Rifles (Berkshire and Wiltshire) Museum, Salisbury.

Chapter four:

On the world stage

Born in 1911 in Independence, Missouri, Virginia Katherine McMath was the iconic star of the silver screen better known as Ginger Rogers.

Her parents separated shortly after her birth and when her mother remarried she took her stepfather's surname of 'Rogers.'

Her forename of 'Ginger' had nothing to do with her hair colour– she adopted it after one of her young relatives who had trouble in pronouncing 'Virginia', called her 'Ginga', later adapted to 'Ginger.'

Not only an actress but also a dancer and singer, she is best remembered for the series of ten musical films she made between 1933 and 1939 with Fred Astaire.

These include the 1933 *Flying Down to Rio*, the 1935 *Top Hat*, the 1936 *Swing Time* and, from 1937, *Shall We Dance*.

Other film roles include the 1940 *Kitty Foyle*, for which she won an Academy Award for Best Actress, the 1945 *Week-End at the Waldorf* and, from 1952, *Monkey Business*.

Ranked fourteenth in the American Film Institutes' 100 Years – 100 Stars list of screen actress legends, she died in 1995.

Not only an actor, but also a humourist and social commentator, **Will Rogers** was one of the world's leading celebrities of the 1920s and 1930s.

Born in 1879 into a Cherokee Nation family in what was then designated as Indian Territory but is now part of Oklahoma, he began his career performing cowboy rope tricks in circuses and then vaudeville.

His many film credits include the 1933 *State Fair* and the 1935 *In Old Kentucky*, while he was also a popular syndicated newspaper columnist.

A supporter of the Democrat Party, he is also famous for a number of witty quips based on his observations of both American politics and life in general.

These include:

"A fool and his money are soon elected" and "There are three kinds of men. The ones that learn by reading. The few who learn by observation. The rest of them have to learn by touching an electric fence."

He was killed in August of 1935 along with the aviator Wiley Post when their small aircraft crashed in Alaska.

Known as "Oklahoma's Favourite Son", the Will Rogers World Airport in Oklahoma City is named in his honour, while he is also a recipient of a star on the Hollywood Walk of Fame.

Born in 1911 in Cincinnati, Leonard Franklin Syle was the American cowboy actor and singer better known as **Roy Rogers**.

It was along with his wife Dale Evans, horse *Trigger* and German shepherd dog *Bullet* that he featured from 1951 to 1957 on television's popular *The Roy Rogers Show*.

Known as "King of the Cowboys" while his wife was "Queen of the West", he also featured in a number of films that include the 1937 *Wild Horse Rodeo*, the 1938 *Under Western Stars* and, from 1940, *The Carson City Kid*. Also known for a string of hit songs that include *A Little White Cross on the Hill* and *My Chickashay Girl*, he died in 1998.

Both he and his wife, who died in 2001, are inductees of the Western Performers Hall of Fame at the National Cowboy and Western Heritage Museum, Colorado City.

On British shores, **Paul Rogers** is the former actor of stage, television and film born in 1917 in Devon.

Winner in 1967 of a Tony Award for Best Actor for his role in playwright Harold Pinter's *The Homecoming*, his screen credits include the 1954 *The Beachcombers*, the 1960 *The Trials of Oscar Wilde* and, from 1969, *The Looking Glass War*.

Back across the Atlantic, **Mimi Rogers**, born Miriam Spickler in 1956 in Coral Gables, Florida, is the American actress whose film credits include the 1986 *Gung Ho* and the 1990 *Desperate Hours*.

Winner of the 2013 Vancouver Film Critics Circle Award for Best Actor in a Canadian Film for his role in *Beyond the Black Rainbow*, **Michael Rogers** is the actor born in 1964 in Victoria, British Columbia. Other film credits include the 2002 *The Dead Zone* and, from 2007, *The Assassination of Jesse James by the Coward Robert Ford*.

Best known for his roles in a number of *Laurel and Hardy* films, **Charley Rogers** was the English actor, director and screenwriter born in 1887 in Birmingham.

Immigrating to the United States, he appeared in nearly 40 films between 1912 and 1954 that include the 1914 *A Ticket to Red Horse Gulch*, the 1929 *Double Whoopee* and, from 1939, *The Flying Deuces*; he died in 1956.

Born in 1934 in Austin, Texas, Betty Jayne Rogers was the American actress better known as **Elizabeth Rogers**.

Known for her role of Lieutenant Palmer, the relief communications officer for Lieutenant Uhuru in the 1960s' television series *Star Trek*, before her death in 2004 her big screen credits included the 1972 *The Poseidon Adventure*, the 1974 *The Towering Inferno* and the 1982 *An Officer and a Gentleman*.

Born in 1904 in Olathe, Kansas, Charles Edward Rogers was the American actor and jazz musician better known as **Buddy Rogers**.

Skilled on a number of musical instruments and performing on both radio and the big screen with his own jazz band, he is best known for having played opposite the actress Clara Bow in the 1927 *Wings* – the first film ever to receive an Academy Award for Best Picture.

With other film credits that include the 1931 *The Road to Rio* and the 1938 *Let's Make a Night of It*, he died in 1999.

Best known as the host from 1978 to 1988 of the popular British television variety game-show 3-2-1, **Ted Rogers** was the comedian and light entertainer born in London in 1935.

Also a regular entertainer on the television show *Sunday Night at the London Palladium*, he died in 2001.

Behind the camera lens, **Peter Rogers**, born in 1914 in Rochester, Kent, and who died in 2009, was the English film producer noted for his involvement in the *Carry On* series of comedy films – beginning in 1958 with *Carry On Sergeant*.

From the stage to the world of music, Kenneth Donald Rogers was the internationally best-selling singer and songwriter better known as **Kenny Rogers**. Born in 1938 in Houston, Texas, and also a record producer and actor, he was famed for hits – some with the band Kenny Rogers and The First Edition – that include *Ruby, Don't Take Your Love to Town*, *Coward of the County*, *Lucille*, *Reuben James*, *Something's Burning* and *The Gambler*.

One of the biggest-selling artists of all time, an inductee of the Country Music Hall of Fame and with acting credits including the television series *The Gambler* and *Rio Diablo*, he died in 2020.

From country music to the blues, **Jimmy Rogers** was the singer, guitarist and harmonica player noted as having been a member during the 1950s of Muddy Waters' band.

Also having enjoyed hits as a solo performer that include his 1945 *Walking By Myself*, he was born James A. Lane in Ruleville, Mississippi, in 1924 and took the stage name 'Rogers' from his stepfather's name; an inductee of the Blues Hall of Fame, he died in 1997.

Born in Detroit in 1940, **Bobby Rogers** was the soul singer and songwriter best known as a member of the Motown band The Miracles, first formed in 1956 and re-named Smokey Robinson and The Miracles in 1965.

Having enjoyed hits with the band that include *Shop Around*, *Bad Girl*, *The Tracks of My Tears* and the 1970 *Tears of a Clown*, he died in 2013.

He was a cousin of fellow band member and singer **Claudette Rogers**, born in 1942 in New Orleans and who became known as Claudette Rogers Robinson following her marriage to Smokey Robinson.

Along with other original members of the band, she is honoured with a star on the Hollywood Walk of Fame.

Recognised as having been one of Canada's greatest ever folk musicians and songwriters, **Stan Rogers** was born in 1949 in Hamilton, Ontario.

With his writing inspired by Canadian history

and the lives of ordinary people, his most famous songs include his 1981 *Northwest Passage*.

He was aged only 33 when, returning to Canada from a music festival in the United States, he was among 23 passengers killed in a fire after Canada Flight 797 was forced to make an emergency landing at Greater Cincinnati Airport, northern Kentucky, after an in-flight fire developed.

He was the older brother of **Garnett Rogers**, the folk musician, singer and songwriter born in 1955 and who used to act as an arranger of his music.

Bearers of the Rogers name have also excelled in the highly competitive world of sport.

Born in 1951 in Waco, Texas, **Bill Rogers** is the American professional golfer who won the 1981 British Open Championship and the Professional Golfers Association (PGA) Grand Slam of Golf a year later.

An inductee of the Canadian Horse Racing Hall of Fame, **Chris Rogers** was the champion jockey born in Hamilton, Ontario, in 1924. He died in 1976 after having enjoyed a string of racing successes that included winning Canada's prestigious race, The Queen's Plate, in 1949, 1950 and 1954.

On the ice rink, **Leigh Rogers**, born in

London in 1989, is the British ice skater who, along with former partner Lloyd Jones, was the British junior national champion in 2006 and 2007.

In the world of the written word, **Byron Rogers**, born in 1942 in Carmarthen, is the Welsh journalist, essayist and biographer whose biography of the Welsh poet and Anglican priest R.S. Thomas, *The Man who Went Into the West*, won Edinburgh University's James Tait Black Memorial Prize for Best Biography in 2007.

A Fellow of the Royal Society of Literature, **Jane Rogers**, born in London in 1952, is the novelist whose *The Testament of Jessie Lamb* was a recipient of an Arthur C. Clarke Award and also long-listed for the 2011 The Man Booker Prize for Fiction.

No account of proud bearers of the Rogers name could perhaps be complete without reference to a famous fictional character.

This is **Buck Rogers**, the space adventurer who made his first appearance in 1928 in the pulp magazine *Amazing Stories* in a tale written by Philip Francis Nowlan. Adapted only a year later for syndicated newspaper comic strips, the bold Buck Rogers has since featured in radio, television and film series in addition to books and video games.